VRIJE UITLOOP | FREE RANGE

Vrije uitloop
———
Free range

POEMS OF
SASKIA STEHOUWER

Translation

+

Field Notes

Joel Thomas Katz

Robert Perry

Saskia Stehouwer

DUTCH POET PRESS
2019

Copyright © 2019 Dutch Poet Press
© 2016 Saskia Stehouwer and Uitgeverij Marmer
All rights reserved.

ISBN Number 978-0-9967056-9-1

Dutch Poet Press
dutchpoetpress.com

PICTURE CREDITS

Cover and interior images:

Indigo, watercolor painting by Elsie Franken-Holt as an Anthroposophical art therapy training exercise with permission from the artist.

Le témoin | De getuige | The witness by herman de vries, born 1931. 64.5 x 238 x 89 cm, trunk of an olive tree, marble (purchased with support from the Mondriaan Foundation) 1991. In the collection of the Kröller-Müller Museum, Otterlo, The Netherlands. © Stichting Kröller-Müller Museum. With permission from the Kröller-Müller Museum and the artist.

Alyssum, photograph by Robert Perry.

Aan de aarde en haar bewoners

To Earth and its inhabitants

PREFACE

We three are seekers of knowledge and beauty walking about the earth as seedpods, leaves, or twigs floating in the air eventually falling to the ground. We are living our lives, pursuing our passions. We love language. We love nature. We love poetry.

It is no surprise we are poet-translators.

We three seekers witness the world we encounter. Each in our own way, we give witness to what we discover in our writing and translation of poetry. In this case from Dutch to English, the poetry by one of us—the book *Vrije uitloop* by Saskia Stehouwer. This is our project. The translation of thirty-four poems with our record of some observations in a section called Field Notes—all designed and published as a book.

This book you are holding in your hands: *Vrije uitloop | Free range*.

How did we find each other? How did the book come to be?

Somehow we met on the lattice of coincidence and began to work together at close quarters and at some distance. Producing a translation of poetry and a collection of essays and poetry together. Two of us Joel Katz and Robert Perry who live in the same city of Palo Alto, California, and one Saskia Stehouwer who lives quite far away in Amsterdam.

Whatever the combination of factors—the provenance of the project, the medium of exchange (in person briefly, by email mostly), the three of us enjoyed working together and what we discovered and shared with one another.

One day we discovered herman de vries and his sculpture *The Witness* on view in the Rietveld Pavilion at the Kröller-Müller Museum in Otterlo, The Netherlands.

We knew right then, at that particular moment, in that particular place, we had found someone and something that spoke to us and gave witness to the nature of our project.

This piece of found art, the trunk of an olive tree, this artifact of nature presented as a work of art placed on a pedestal, put in our path for us to discover and find special meaning in it. Our book like the sculpture is nature serving as a work of art. Our book like the sculpture is offering witness—it is showing, not telling how we human beings and nature are part of the same whole. We are connected within the same ecosystem, a process of exchange and transformation. Just like our project and our experience of the sculpture.

An equilibrium that is dynamic.

In our book with the poems of Saskia and in the sculpture of herman, we discovered:

Nature as Witness. Art as Witness. Artist as Witness.

++++

We three continue to ask in wonder: How did this happen? What made this possible?

We continue to discover other marvels ever more intriguing.

The entry way of the Kröller-Müller Museum has had a bright

colorful sculpture by Bruce Nauman that declares in a spiral of neon letters: "the true artist helps the world by revealing mystic truths".

Joel Katz, our fellow poet-translator friend on this project, revealed to us his favorite Dutch word is *getuige* … witness.

Both herman de vries and Saskia Stehouwer were born in the same place—Alkmaar, a small city in northern Holland.

The sculpture *The Witness* by herman de vries resembles closely the driftwood pieces seen in California. They are often put on display as sculpture and appear in the photographs of Ansel Adams and Edward Weston. They have become icons of the California coast and prominent in the thoughts of Joel and Robert.

All to say that herman's sculpture became emblematic of our collaboration and exchange between a *Nederlander* (born and raised in the countryside) and two Californians. This amazing discovery led us to put an image of the sculpture on the front and back cover of our book.

In addition to our embrace of *The Witness*, the three of us have begun to wander and explore the entire field of his art work produced over six decades. We have become absorbed in his wonderous open-air cabinet of curiosities.

We are struck by the thought that our book project does not end when it is published. Like nature, the process is open and dynamic and ongoing. Our project miraculously renews itself with new life as the book circulates in the world like a seedpod, leaf, or twig, as it finds itself in someone's garden.

CONTENTS

PREFACE ix

POEMS

grasmaaiers | lawnmowers	
duizend manieren om mens te zijn |	4
a thousand ways to be human	
hoogtevrees | fear of heights	6
afslaan | exit	8
vast | fixed	10
grijs gebied | gray area	12
kloof | cleft	14
jacht | hunt	16
brief aan onze overzeese lezers |	18
letter to our overseas readers	
je schip laten invriezen en aan boord blijven |	
let your ship freeze over and stay on board	
verhalen over zij | stories about they	22
ik hang rond in een niemandsland |	24
I hang around in a no man's land	
in de wolken | in the clouds	26
wortels | roots	28
windstil | windless	30
opties | options	32
jonge ogen | young eyes	36
laat me je tweede helft zien |	38
let me see your second half	
wachtzet |waiting move	40
kabel | cable	42

achter de waterval | behind the waterfall	44

de tijd schaft niet \| time doesn't take a break

document | document	48
van voorbij de akker | from beyond the farm field	50
medaille | medal	52
daadzaken | a matter of deeds	56
gang | passage	58
scherm | screen	60
samenloop | convergence	62

padvinders \| pathfinders

gans worden | becoming goose	66
het licht in het water | the light in the water	70
viool | violin	72
bij | bee	74
in de coulissen | in the wings	76
het rumoer van zomaar een lichaam | the noise of just a body	78
schutting | fence	80
voor de boeg | ahead of the prow	82

FIELD NOTES

Writing Bewilderment into Wonder by Saskia Stehouwer	87
For a new year by Joel Thomas Katz	90
Parables of Consciousness: Guide to *Vrije uitloop* by Saskia Stehouwer by Robert Perry	91

Het Spreekwoord & Saskia Stehouwer by Saskia Stehouwer	95
About Ecopoetry by Joel Thomas Katz	96
Indigo: Crisis of Good Intentions by Robert Perry	101
A Conversation: Poet-Translators of *Vrije uitloop* Joel Thomas Katz, Robert Perry, and Saskia Stehouwer	103
Alyssum by Robert Perry	128

TRANSLATION NOTES 129

ACKNOWLEDGMENTS 131

COLOPHON 135

GEDICHTEN | POEMS

grasmaaiers

lawnmowers

duizend manieren om mens te zijn

wij staken een duif de ogen uit
hingen hem aan een paal
om zijn soortgenoten te weren

we schoten buffels neer
tot het winter werd op de vlaktes

we bezochten plekken tot ze verbleekten
en begonnen af te geven

we vergaten hoe een boom groeit

kan ik hier geboren worden
als het zand de verkeerde kant op waait
en de kevers de weg kwijt zijn

wil ik komen luisteren naar een kring van mensen
die niet weten wat ze moeten doen
met de resten

een keel werd doorgesneden
het litteken is te zien

a thousand ways to be human

we poked out the eyes of a dove
hung him on a pole
to deter his kind

we shot down buffalo
until it was winter on the plains

we visited places until they faded
and began to give up color

we forgot how a tree grows

can I be born here
if the sand blows in the wrong direction
and the beetles are lost

do I want to listen to a circle of people
who don't know what they should do
with the remains

a throat got slit
the scar is visible

hoogtevrees

ik zit op de tafel in een flat en eet een appel
ik woon hier zonder te weten waarom
is er iemand die met me mee wil lopen?

tussen de plek waar je nog kunt komen
voor je benzine op is
en het punt waarop het weer lukt
om het pedaal in te drukken
roeren zich de verborgen dingen

ik strek me uit tot mijn kleren afvallen
en de tafel me niet meer kan zien
van verveling begin ik te bloeden

het verleden belt op spreekt in
had je een vriend besteld?

onraad is niet de beer op de weg
maar de rat in mijn brein
die veel beter kauwt
en er de tijd voor neemt

fear of heights

I sit on the table in a flat and eat an apple
I live here without knowing why
is there someone who wants to walk with me?

between the place you can still reach
before you run out of gas
and the point when you manage
to press the pedal again
hidden things begin to stir

I stretch myself until my clothes fall off
and the table no longer sees me
boredom makes me bleed

the past phones up leaves a message
did you order a friend?

trouble is not the bear on the road
but the rat in my brain
that chews properly
and takes its time

afslaan

hij wil geen koers bepalen
maar zich vriendelijk losmaken
van de verkopers
ze vertellen hun verhaal
dwars door hem heen

hij stelt zich een reiziger voor

via het geluid van een zaag die zijn hoofd aansnijdt
tuimelt hij het zoveelste toekomstperspectief in
zijn leven glad als de huid van een tuinboon

een stropdas voor de avonden waarop hij bijna uitgaat
om dan alsnog te verkruimelen
een grote hoed voor de toeristenwijk
waar hij steeds schuin doorheen wandelt
alsof hij zich wil verontschuldigen

zijn geest de lenige fooienteller in het restaurant
die er met de buit vandoor wil

er zit een wesp op zijn locale specialiteit
een winkelwagen ligt gewond op de stoep

het is geen dag om een taal te leren

exit

he wants to chart no course
but amiably detach himself
from the vendors
they tell their story
right through him

he pictures a traveler

through the sound of a saw that cuts into his head
he tumbles into yet another perspective
his life smooth as the skin of a broad bean

a necktie for the evenings when he almost goes out
only to crumble instead
a big hat for the tourist area
that he keeps angling through
as if wanting to apologize

his mind the nimble tip collector in the restaurant
who wants to make off with the loot

there's a wasp on his local specialty
a shopping cart lies on the sidewalk wounded

it's no day to learn a language

vast

in je precieze jaren
toen je zelden buitenkwam
omdat je onder schot stond
zagen maar weinig mensen
hoe wit je haar was

als ik door de glazen deur kijk
zie ik een trillend been

we gaan graven
met de resten van een lange dag
aan onze vingers

wijzen plekken aan waar onkruid groeit
laten de thee onze tong vormen

als we de jassen aantrekken
bevriezen onze voeten

we zwieren op het ijs
tussen de hopeloos zwalkende honden
op zoek naar een lijn een bal een bot

we zullen weer naar school gaan
we zullen naar een winkel rijden
omdat het prettig is om iets te kopen
voor het op is

fixed

in your years of precision
when you rarely came outside
because you were held at gunpoint
few people got to see
how white your hair was

as I look through the glass door
I see a leg shaking

we go digging
with the remains of a long day
on our fingers

point out places where weeds grow
let the tea shape our tongue

as we put on the coats
our feet freeze

we whirl on the ice
between the hopelessly lurching dogs
seeking a rope a ball a bone

we'll go back to school again
we'll drive to a store
because it's nice to buy something
before it's gone

grijs gebied

je legt je vertakte hand op het papier
wijst een wegrennend woord aan

zwart de smeer van mijn gedachten
die zich verstoppen achter je broche

we ruiken de ellenlange groenten
die door oude magen glijden

de knikkebollende kruiswoordpuzzels
de joelende tv

de oortjesstoel die zich schikt
naar je krimpende hoofd
als je een tukje doet

vangt je zweet op
draagt je benen

het is zachter dan juichen
alleen als je luistert
verheft het zijn stem

gray area

you lay your gnarled hand on the paper
point out a word running away

black the grease of my thoughts
that hide behind your brooch

we smell the endless vegetables
gliding through old stomachs

the crossword puzzles nodding off
the whooping tv

the wing chair that conforms
to your shrinking head
when you take a nap

captures your sweat
carries your legs

it is softer than cheering
only if you listen
does it raise its voice

kloof

voordat je de put opent
is het handig om te weten
hoe je een ladder afdaalt

besmette randen
hier heeft een dier gelekt

twee handen in een wit veld
harken naar wortels

twee jurken en een dagboek
hangen aan de waslijn

schoon wordt het niet meer

je opent het deksel
ziet geen ladder
de geur zet je op een lopen

cleft

before you open the pit
it's useful to know
how to climb down a ladder

contaminated edges
an animal has leaked here

two hands in a white field
rake for roots

two dresses and a diary
hang on the clothesline

things won't get clean anymore

you open the lid
see no ladder
the smell sets you off running

jacht

het mooiste ontwerp voor een hamer is gebaseerd
op de snavel van een specht
de beste airco imiteert de wijze waarop zebra's
warmte geleiden door hun lichaam

hij droomt ervan het einde te zien

de regen die de geluiden aan elkaar knoopt
de wind die de regendruppels optilt

hij aarzelt voor hij voet in de witte gymschoen
op de royale neushoornnek zet
glimlacht voor de foto
niemand kent hem hier

+++

we blazen de bomen uit elkaar
zodat een pad ontstaat
waarlangs mensen uit het verleden
worden binnengehaald

we hebben allemaal een eigen geur
verstoppen ons in een hoek van de nacht
tot iemand brullend een heuvel afrent

angst is rust die nog niet begrepen wordt

hunt

the best design for a hammer is based
on the beak of a woodpecker
the best air conditioning imitates the way zebras
conduct heat through their bodies

he dreams of seeing the end

the rain that ties the sounds together
the wind that lifts up the raindrops

he hesitates before placing his white-sneakered foot
on the lavish rhino neck
smiles for the photo
nobody knows him here

+++

we blow the trees apart
to create a path
along which people from the past
are brought in

we all have our own scent
hide in a corner of the night
until someone runs down a hill roaring

fear is peace not yet understood

brief aan onze overzeese lezers

nu zijn wij degenen
die onze spullen dragen
naar de huizen van vrienden
die verdwijnen in de achterzak
van de tussenpersoon

nu zijn wij degenen
die aan boord gaan
om te varen over een zee
waarvan we het einde niet kennen

ooit zijn jullie degenen
die warme kleren aantrekken
die aarzelend kennismaken

hoe lang blijven we samen

nu zijn wij degenen
die het onze moeders niet vertellen
die onze kinderen kalmeren
voordoen hoe ze moeten zwemmen

straks zijn wij degenen
die rustig slapen
in ons nieuwe huis
op jullie bodem

letter to our overseas readers

now we're the ones
carrying our gear
to the homes of friends
and disappearing into the back pocket
of the middleman

now we're the ones
going on board
to sail on a sea
whose end we don't know

someday you'll be the ones
putting on warm clothes
and meeting hesitantly

how long will we be together

now we're the ones
not telling our mothers
and calming our children
by teaching them how to swim

soon we'll be the ones
sleeping peacefully
in our new house
on your ground

je schip laten invriezen
en aan boord blijven

let your ship freeze over
and stay on board

verhalen over zij

het land waar je eerder leert schieten dan spreken
zit om de tafel met het land waar je bloedgroep bepaalt
of je een baan krijgt of het raam uitspringt
samen met het land waarvan de president
acht keer getrouwd is
en het land dat gevangenen eerder vrijlaat als ze boeken lezen
ze hebben het over de landen waar de vrouwen
zich zo bedekt mogelijk opstellen
en de landen waar mensen hun dieren verven

er schuift een leeg land aan
de inwoners zijn vertrokken naar het land
waar de diesel van de groene muren druipt
of naar het land dat in staking gaat
als de inwoners een week later met pensioen moeten

wij zijn er ook
wij zien het hoofdschuddend aan
wij weten het beter

stories about they

the country where you learn to shoot before you learn
    to speak
sits around the table with the country where your blood-type
    determines
whether you get a job or jump out the window
together with the country whose president
has been married eight times
and the country that releases its prisoners early when they
    read books
they are talking about the countries where the women
cover themselves as much as possible
and the countries where people dye their animals

an empty country joins in
the residents have left for the country
where diesel fuel drips from the green walls
or for the country that goes on strike
when its residents' retirement age goes up by one week

we are there too
we watch shaking our heads
we know better

ik hang rond in een niemandsland
waar douaniers hun middagdutje doen
ik ga voorlopig nergens heen
dus kom maar op met je verhaal

ditmaal ga ik echt iets doen
want we delen een land
want mijn kleinzoon
zit op dezelfde voetbalclub
want mijn tante heeft ook kanker

ik ga met een kleine gieter het bos in
en kom drie geiten tegen

zie het kwaad
hoor het kwaad
en zeg het voort

natuurlijk moeten ze geholpen worden
maar we wonen in een klein dorp
en de sfeer moet goed blijven

jij bent de enige die nog beweegt
de rest is bezaaid en ingemaakt

I'm hanging around in a no-man's-land
where customs officers are taking their afternoon nap
I won't be going anywhere for a while
so bring on your story

this time I'm really going to do something
because we share a country
because my grandson
plays on the same soccer team
because my aunt also has cancer

I take a small watering-can into the woods
and come upon three goats

see the evil
hear the evil
put it out there

of course they should be helped
but we live in a small village
and the atmosphere needs to stay pleasant

you're the only one who is still moving
the rest are sown and preserved

in de wolken

mensen op vensterbanken
mensen op richels met tasjes
mensen met dekens om zich heen

omdat het gelukt is
omdat het niet gelukt is

spraken op gedempte toon
uitten hun zorgen over de baby
spanden een vangnet

de verlaten ogen
de nette kleren

iedereen weer heelhuids beneden
sommigen omhelsd
anderen weggehaald

kan aandacht onder hun huid komen
of voedt die de schrokkerige schaamte
die alleen op hoogte geen honger heeft

in the clouds

people on windowsills
people on ledges with purses
people with blankets wrapped around them

because they succeeded
because they didn't succeed

spoke in hushed tones
voiced their concerns about the baby
spread a safety net

the abandoned eyes
the neat clothes

everyone down again in one piece
some hugged
others taken away

can attention get under their skin
or does it feed the ravenous shame
that only on high is not hungry

wortels

ik keer terug naar de knoop in de straten
tot de herhaling een nieuwe weg oplevert

mensen denken dat ik niet meer groei
maar ik loop door onder de grond
langs het hol van de sluipwesp en de rioolbuizen
tot waar het warm wordt

ik laat mijn voeten smelten en bestel nieuwe
kom weer boven voor het eten

thuis liggen mijn ogen nog op het nachtkastje
ze raken minder van slag
als ze muren kunnen zien

ik blijf hameren op hetzelfde stuk staal
dat steeds zwijgzamer wordt

roots

I return to the knot in the streets
until the recurrence yields a new path

people think I no longer grow
but I continue underground
along the cave of the scorpion wasp and the sewer pipes
toward where it gets warm

I let my feet melt and order new ones
come back up for dinner

at home my eyes still lie on the nightstand
they get less upset
if they can see walls

I keep hammering on the same piece of steel
which is becoming more and more taciturn

windstil

de ochtend verloopt zo eigenaardig
dat haar man vergeet vreemd te gaan
en de hond overgeeft in de keuken

de buurman eist een onderhoud
zijn kippen leggen in de verkeerde tuin
dat had voorkomen moeten worden

het achternichtje staat pruilend op de stoep
omdat de lippenstift thuis op is

ze trekt zich terug in een hoek van de bank
gehuld in de vodden van haar goede eigenschappen
strijkt haar eten glad met een vork

mensen die haar op straat hebben gezien
zeggen dat haar tempo eigenlijk heel hoog ligt

windless

the morning goes by so peculiarly
that her husband forgets to cheat on her
and the dog throws up in the kitchen

the neighbor demands a meeting
his hens are laying eggs in the wrong garden
this should have been prevented

the distant cousin stands pouting on the sidewalk
because she has run out of lipstick at home

she retreats into a corner of the sofa
wrapped in the rags of her good qualities
smooths her food with a fork

people who have seen her on the street
say that her pace is actually quite brisk

opties

denk je dat er iets aan de hand is
dat het galmen van de klokken
iets te betekenen heeft

vroeger voelde ik me veilig
als er iemand thuis was
het enige dat 's nachts openstond
het raam in mijn hoofd

ik vond een complot in het gekakel van meeuwen
bleef binnen de stoeptegels
er was een jongen die mij graag sloeg
waardoor ik nu een oog op mijn rug draag

nu je het zegt

het zat gisteren dicht
dat moet toch verband houden
met het stuk ijzerdraad in mijn hand
en de geur van de zalf van mijn oma
die vanmiddag ineens voorbij dreef

allemaal deuren naar dezelfde ruimte

options

do you think something is the matter
that the pealing of bells
means something

I used to feel safe
if there was someone at home
the only thing open at night was
the window in my head

I found a conspiracy in the cackle of seagulls
stayed within the paving stones
there was a boy who liked to hit me
so now I wear an eye on my back

now that you mention it

yesterday it was closed
that should be related somehow
to the piece of wire in my hand
and the smell of my grandma's salve
which suddenly floated past me this afternoon

all doors to the same space

dorpsgenoten in de avond
schreeuwen en lossen schoten
ik hoest wat harder
kijk je al?

pas als ik word ingestopt
kan ik zonder handen fietsen
verschijnt er een oprijlaan voor mijn huis

in the evening villagers
shout and fire shots
I cough a bit harder
are you looking yet?

only when I'm tucked in
can I ride a bike without hands
does a lane appear in front of my house

jonge ogen

stem omhoog   kop omlaag

ik wil je vertellen hoe lelijk je bent
je handen te groot voor mijn planten
je voeten rolluiken voor mijn huis
ik vertel je hoe lelijk ik ben

iemand die nog niet bestaat
loopt over mijn typelint
ik loop hem achterna
kom jou opnieuw tegen

je handen een hartslagmonitor
die de letters aan elkaar naait
je voeten balanceren op de punt van mijn tong
zeilboten in mijn hoofd

ik bouw een huis waarin je tekeer kunt gaan
het raam waardoor de wind
naar binnen gluurt ben ik

waar zullen we zijn als ze ons vinden
wat laten we achter in hun handen
nergens in mijn lichaam zit iets wat op mij lijkt

toen ik gisteren bloemen kocht
wist ik niet dat ze voor jou waren

young eyes

voice up   head down

I want to tell you how ugly you are
your hands too big for my plants
your feet roll-down shutters for my house
I tell you how ugly I am

someone who does not yet exist
moves across my typewriter ribbon
I go after him
come across you again

your hands a heart-rate monitor
that sews the letters together
your feet balancing on the tip of my tongue
sailboats in my head

I build a house in which you can rampage
the window through which the wind
peeks inside is me

where will we be when they find us
what do we leave behind in their hands
nowhere in my body is anything resembling me

yesterday when I bought flowers
I didn't know they were for you

laat me je tweede helft zien

toen ik behoefte had aan een klein wonder
was het koud maar goed weer
sprong een hert over de weg
zaten er mensen in het café

mijn vrouw bedenkt wat ik zeg
als logisch uitvloeisel van ons huwelijk

wil je dat soms even op het bord schrijven?

wij denken dat we binnen alles onder controle hebben
behalve het kierende water en de zingende muizen
zo flinterdun dat we er op een heldere dag
doorheen kunnen kijken

wat betekent het om echt te kiezen
een deur te sluiten omdat de lucht je tegen staat
een sleutel neer te leggen waar je hem zult vergeten

let me see your second half

when I needed a small miracle
the weather was cold but good
a deer jumped across the road
there were people in the cafe

my wife thinks up what I say
as a logical consequence of our marriage

maybe you want to write that on the board?

we think that inside we have everything under control
except for the water breaking through and the singing mice
so paper-thin that on a clear day
we can see through it

what does it mean to have real choice
to shut a door because the air smells bad
to set a key down where you'll forget it

wachtzet

jij valt pas aan als het werk af is
houdt je middenveld bezet
leerde het spel tot het ophield een spel te zijn

een gevecht dat je in een adem kunt voeren
dat je kunt winnen zonder aanwezig te zijn

je maakt een rondje langs de soldaten
weet van wie de voet trilt
voor wie de bepakking te zwaar is
en wie niet tegen verrassingen kan

je leert anderen vooruit te denken

rond je kamp pakt de spanning zich samen
manschappen nemen hun posities in
tegenstanders schoppen onder tafel

je zet je legers klaar voor de nacht
sluit het luik in je hoofd

het is hun beurt

waiting move

you attack when the work is done
keep your midfield occupied
you learned the game until it stopped being a game

a fight you can handle in one breath
that you can win without being there

you make the rounds before the troops
know whose foot trembles
whose pack is too heavy
and who cannot handle surprises

you teach others to think ahead

tension gathers through your camp
soldiers take up their positions
opponents kicking under the table

you ready your armies for the night
shut the hatch in your head

it's their turn

kabel

dus sta ik daar op de berg iets te verkondigen
om jou nog verder te verbeteren

jij moet nog het verkeer in
je mag nergens spijt van hebben

ik zal eens opletten of ik muziek kan horen

de hele zondag mag je bewegen
voor het goede doel

op de loopband voor je volgende avontuur
meters maken bij een paar graden onder nul

toen kwam pia en zijn we maar gaan verbouwen
een beetje uit verhouding allemaal

jij hebt jaren niet geschaakt
omdat ik daar nogal op aandrong

nu doe je zetten die onbegrijpelijk zijn

cable

so I'm standing there on the mountain to declare something
that will improve you even more

you must still hit the road
you should have no regrets

I'll pay attention if I can hear music

all sunday you get to move
for a good cause

on the treadmill for your next adventure
clocking some miles at a couple of grades below zero

then came pia and we went about remodeling
all a bit out of proportion

you haven't played chess for years
because I pretty much insisted on it

now you're making moves that are incomprehensible

achter de waterval

begin achter een struik in de tuin
kijk steeds verder het donker in

de kracht die de dag van de nacht scheidt
de kracht die slaapt maar op wil staan
de kracht die de golven naar zich toetrekt
om de nacht te verlichten

ons oude zonlicht oogsten
onze olie gebruiken
als we eigenlijk willen slapen

iemand is een sterrenstelsel
iemand heeft geen goede avond
iemand is een zwart gat

als je het ons vraagt op de verkeerde dag zeggen we ja

wees alert op verwarde mensen
teken een cirkel rond een lijk
blijf drie dagen kijken
tot het evenwicht terugkeert

het gaat niet over jou
maar leg dat jezelf maar eens uit

behind the waterfall

start behind a bush in the garden
look even further into the dark

the power that separates day from night
the power that sleeps but wants to get up
the power that pulls the waves toward itself
to lighten up the night

to harvest our old sunlight
use our oil
when all we really want to do is sleep

someone is a galaxy
someone does not have a good evening
someone is a black hole

if you ask us on the wrong day we say yes

be alert for confused people
draw a circle around a corpse
keep looking for three days
until the balance returns

it's not about you
but try explaining that to yourself

de tijd schaft niet

time doesn't take a break

document

het kleinkind van de familie abramovic
zit op een verdriet dat niet van hem is
een verdriet dat de eigenaars terug willen

als je al jaren goed werk levert
kunnen ze je dan accepteren
of moet je iets over hun wereld zeggen
waardoor die wereld voor hun ogen verandert

ik merk dat ik hier tijdens wandelingen vaak aan denk
hoe zeg ik iets dat de wereld verandert in de wereld
die ik wil zien

het kleinkind van de familie abramovic heeft te korte wortels
bij elk stormpje waait hij om
als hij opkrabbelt is hij vergeten waar hij stond
en kan hij niets zeggen dat de wereld verandert
omdat zijn wereld zich zonder zijn toedoen verplaatst
en de wereld van zijn voorouders tot stilstand is gekomen

zonder schouders blijven zij rechtop staan
wantrouwen het kleinkind dat niets gezien heeft
willen zorgen dat hij nooit iets te zien krijgt
en zwijgen

document

the grandchild of the abramovic family
sits on a sorrow not his own
a sorrow which the owners want back

if you've been doing a good job for many years
then can they accept you
or should you say something about their world
through which this world changes before their eyes

I notice that I think about this often during walks
how can I say something that changes the world
into the world that I want to see

the grandchild of the abramovic family has roots that are
    too short
with every little storm he's blown over
as he struggles to get up he's forgotten where he stood
and there's nothing he can say that changes the world
because his world shifts without his doing anything
and the world of his ancestors has come to a standstill

without shoulders they remain standing upright
distrust the grandchild who hasn't seen anything
want to be careful that he never gets to see anything
and are silent

van voorbij de akker

toen we iets langs in onszelf ontdekten
wisten we dat we voorbij de taal moesten
op de bast van de boom in de tuin
veegden we de schilfers op
voegden ze samen met de lijm van onze aandacht

we verlieten het dorp met spijt in onze ogen
en grond onder onze nagels
omdat we verwacht werden

liepen voor ons leven
met een aktentas en een vogelkooi
zo sterk als de zwakste schakel
hielden elkaar vast bij de enkel
want lager dan de grond kun je niet

bleven steeds waakzaam
want je neus slaapt ook

al die dromen over een lang leven
terwijl het erom gaat dat je ergens aankomt
waar iemand je uit de menigte plukt

help ons om er te komen
help ons op het hoofd te klimmen
om de gedachten te zien

from beyond the farm field

when we discovered a tall something within us
we knew we had to go beyond the language
on the bark of the tree in the garden
we swept up the slivers
put them together with the glue of our attention

we left the village with regret in our eyes
and dirt under our nails
because we were expected

ran for our lives
with a briefcase and a bird cage
as strong as the weakest link
held each other at the ankle
because you can't go lower than the ground

always stayed vigilant
because your nose sleeps too

all those dreams about a long life
while it's about arriving somewhere
where someone plucks you out of the crowd

help us to get there
help us to climb up the head
to see the thoughts

medaille

onder de huid van de wereld
kruip je rond op zoek naar voedsel

wij durven je niet te onderbreken
omdat je vrouw overleden is

op reis om te laten zien dat je het echt meent
op reis omdat je thuis niet genoeg kunt doen
op reis om het geloof in jezelf te omzeilen

in een rivier liggen veel stenen
gebruik ze allemaal

+++

we benaderen het even van de andere kant

je maakt nu deel uit van de groep
die je voorheen zo ijverig bestudeerde

er nadert een vraag over jou

je oordelen vliegen alle kanten op
nu ze het touwtje van de afstand
met hun scherpe nagels
hebben losgepeuterd

medal

under the skin of the world
you crawl around looking for food

we dare not interrupt you
because your wife died

travel to show you really mean it
travel because you can't do enough at home
travel to avoid believing in yourself

in a river there are many stones
use them all

+++

let's approach it from the other side for a minute

you are now part of the group
that you studied so diligently before

a question about you arises

your judgments are shattered all over the place
now they have loosened
the string of distance
with their sharp nails

de stapelbedden van je vrees
waar je schaduw niet langer
achter een muurtje kan gaan staan

gisteren verhuisde je buurvrouw
omdat ze al haar meubels had verbrand
toen ze niet meer wist wie ze was

the bunkbeds of your fear
where your shadow can no longer
stay behind a wall

yesterday your neighbor moved away
because she had burned up all her furniture
when she no longer knew who she was

daadzaken

ik vertrouw de weg niet die ik insloeg
met een hongerig oog en weke voeten
de boot gromt nog na in de verte
en uit de vegetatie valt niets af te lezen

het eten van gisteren was een slechte raadgever
mijn darmen kwaakten als kikkers in de nacht

ik heb een nieuw kompas nodig
niet die vuile ster die me aangrijnst
of de rokerige luchtspiegelingen
de kisten in ons hoofd
waarin we langzaam verdwijnen

mijn vader was de sterkste man in de haven
en mijn moeder huilde nooit
ik moet dus in staat zijn
om een reisplan op te stellen

als ik later terugkijk
wil ik geen schedel zien
met hangende tanden

ik zet de toon
ik denk het wonder uit het water

a matter of deeds

I don't trust the path I took
with a hungry eye and soggy feet
the boat still grumbles in the distance
and nothing can be read from the vegetation

yesterday's food was a piece of bad advice
my gut croaked like frogs in the night

I need a new compass
not that foul star that grins at me
or the smoky mirages
the boxes in our head
in which we slowly disappear

my father was the strongest man in the harbor
and my mother never cried
so I have to be able
to draw up a travel plan

when I look back later
I do not want to see a skull
with teeth hanging

I set the tone
I think the miracle out of the water

gang

je brengt me naar buiten
waar ik in het gras kan zitten
het jaar kan horen dat op gang komt

de droom zet in op dezelfde plek
kijkt me nog niet aan

ik begin te bewegen
in de richting van een deur
kan nog geen kleuren zien

dan komt het moment om iets te zeggen
waardoor mijn vingers open gaan
en de omtrek voelen van de klink

half zo oud zit ik naast je
mijn vingers oefenen bewegingen
waarin ik later zal wonen

het is mijn laaste dag met de spoken
morgen ga ik ergens heen
waar ik zal leren dat ze niet bestaan

passage

you bring me outside
where I can sit on the grass
can hear the year that's starting up

the dream begins at the same spot
doesn't look at me yet

I start to move
in the direction of a door
still can't see any colors

then comes the moment to say something
that will cause my fingers to open
and feel the contour of the latch

half as old I sit next to you
my fingers practicing movements
that I'll later come to inhabit

it's my last day with the ghosts
tomorrow I go someplace else
where I'll learn that they don't exist

scherm

ik droomde van M vannacht
hij stond voor het laatst op de middenstip
en dirigeerde met zijn ogen
de jonge spelers naar het doel

toen de draden in zijn hoofd
hun eigen weg begonnen te gaan
stond ik klaar met een handdoek
voor als hij het warm kreeg
en zichzelf onbedoeld zonder kleren vond

vannacht was ik weer bij M
de verhalen gleden door mijn vingers zijn trui in
hij glimlachte toen ik dacht aan de baljurken van tante G
aan de kruidendranken die we brouwden
en die keer dat ik op een bierflesje was gaan staan
en lachend een rood spoor trok naar huis

we vielen in slaap

toen ik wakker werd
legde ik zijn trui op het dak
voor de vogels
huurde een brommer
om door het weiland te rijden

screen

I dreamed of M tonight
he stood at the center spot
and with his eyes directed
the young players toward the goal

when the wiring in his head
started to go its own way
I stood ready with a towel
in case he got warm
and would inadvertently find himself without clothes

tonight I was with M again
the stories slipped through my fingers into his sweater
he smiled when I thought of the ball gowns of Auntie G
of the herbal teas we brewed
and of the time I had stood on a beer bottle
and laughing left a red trail all the way home

we fell asleep

when I woke up
I put his sweater on the roof
for the birds
rented a moped
to drive through the fields

samenloop

om je heen werd geklaagd over files
deden mensen haastig boodschappen
om op tijd thuis te zijn voor de kinderen

een overmoedige vogel begon aan een nest

bijna niemand zag jou liggen
en jij zag bijna niemand meer

herinneringen trokken aan je haar
bewogen mee met de wind
die je opnam in zijn verzameling

wie stilstaat wordt een rood licht
waar anderen doorheen razen

convergence

around you there were complaints about traffic
people were doing their errands in a hurry
to get home in time for the children

an overconfident bird began a nest

hardly anyone saw you lying there
and you saw almost no one anymore

memories pulled at your hair
moved along with the wind
that included you in its collection

if you stand still you become a red light
that others race through

padvinders

pathfinders

gans worden

op je knieën in het water gaan zitten
je armen intrekken en wegstoppen
langs je zij

je bovenlijf als een lobbige saus
over je dijbenen laten lopen

peddelen met je voeten
tot je langzaam omhoog komt

je nek uitsteken en je voortanden
verzagen

schouderbladen niet langer de grens

nog hoger de nek
tot je over jezelf heen kunt kijken

dobberen en schor schreeuwen
dat je een bewaker bent

en achter dit alles
weten dat je weg kunt

dat je dit lichaam kunt meenemen
tree voor tree omhoog
naar het draaihek van de lucht

becoming goose

go sit with your knees in the water
retracting your arms and tucking them
along your side

your upper body running over your thighs
like a heavy sauce

paddling with your feet
until you slowly come up

sticking out your neck and sawing up
your front teeth

shoulder blades no longer the limit

the neck higher still
until you can look out over yourself

bobbing and hoarsely screaming
that you're a guardian

and behind all this
knowing you can get away

that you can take this body with you
step by step upward
to the turnstile of the sky

het zijn niet je gedachten die stijgen
het is de wind die van richting verandert
het blad dat naast je neerploft in het water
het nest dat zich vormt in je buik

je ongeboren kinderen die weten
wanneer het tijd is om te gaan

it's not your thoughts that rise
it's the wind that changes direction
the leaf that plops into the water next to you
the nest that forms in your belly

your unborn children who know
when it's time to go

het licht in het water

ik spreek een man in zijn laatste fase
hij heeft weinig nodig

ik zie in het park een jonge hond
happen naar zijn start

iemand schrijft dat we nog snel
een doos moeten komen halen
voor hij er niet meer is

een kind wordt geboren
een kind houdt stand in een buik

ik trap een zware motor aan
ik schop mijn schoenen uit
en voel waar de straat begint

the light in the water

I talk to a man in his final phase
he has few needs

I see a young dog in the park
chasing its tail

somebody writes that we must quickly
come and pick up a box
before he is gone

a child is born
a child holds out in a belly

I crank up a heavy motor
I kick off my shoes
and feel where the street begins

viool

de boom zit in de vogel
in de darmen van de vis
voelt zich thuis

in het dienende water
het verlangen naar water

zoals de koe haar melk nakijkt
als die de emmer vult
de melk in de emmer
is niet de melk in de koe

de lente klimt uit de snaren
van de groene speler
lianen wenken naar een lege stam
voor een ongestoord verblijf

de speler zit in de vogels
die hun vleugels samenknijpen
om geluid te maken

ze krijgen hun muziek door van de takken
van de boom die in de vis zit
en zich daar thuisvoelt

violin

the tree is in the bird
in the bowels of the fish
feels at home

in the serving water
the desire for water

just like the cow looks at her milk
as it fills the pail
the milk in the pail
is not the milk in the cow

spring climbs out of the strings
of the green player
lianas point to an empty tree trunk
for an undisturbed stay

the musician is in the birds
who squeeze their wings together
to make sound

they catch their music from the branches
of the tree that is in the fish
and feels at home there

bij

binnen een week moet ons kind zich vullen
om het volk te kunnen dienen
wie niet deugt wordt er uitgedooid

wij kennen onze kast
vliegen nooit verkeerd

soms vertrekt het halve volk
om aan een boom te gaan hangen
kauwend op de keuze
tussen werk en dood

zonder ons geen eten
zonder ons een stap terug

we kruipen tegen elkaar aan
blazen onze borst op
als verwarming

aan het eind verdelen we de resten
zodat iedereen tegelijk sterft

bee

within a week our child must fill himself up
to be able to serve the people
whoever isn't fit gets thrown out

we know our hive
never fly the wrong way

sometimes half the group leaves
to go hang on a tree
chewing on the choice
between work and death

without us no food
without us a step back

we crawl against each other
puff up our chest
for warmth

at the end we divide what remains
so that everyone dies at the same time

in de coulissen

als zijn voeten horen
dat de grond terugpraat
komen de kuddes

hij houdt de wacht over degenen
die de wolven op tijd laten huilen
tegen de indringer die de weg ontdekt

de anderen wonen hier alleen
hun handen net sterk genoeg
om het leven te dragen
ze verwarmen hun gedachten
worden stiller tijdens het verdampen

bij de ingang zijn stem die zegt
ze vervliegen en ze keren weer terug
als parasieten naar hun gastheer

hij geeft zijn botten een zetje
en beweegt zich naar de poort
waarachter ze vol ongeduld
op hem wachten

in the wings

when his feet hear
that the ground is talking back
the herds are coming

he stands watch over the ones
who let the wolves howl on time
against the intruder who finds the way

the others merely reside here
their hands just strong enough
to carry life
they warm their thoughts
becoming quieter while they evaporate

at the entrance his voice that says
they disappear and they return again
like parasites to their host

he gives his bones a shove
and moves himself to the gate
behind which they wait for him
most impatiently

het rumoer van zomaar een lichaam

je bent op je best
als je ziet waar je staat

je hart de trommel van je wijsgeer
die het beter weet maar niet kan praten
rondstampt zoals de dikke bovenbuurman
op weg naar oplossingen in de koelkast

rol je verhaal op
en leg het naast je neer

in de dans zit een moment
waarop de dansers niet bewegen
maar de dans doorgaat in hun ogen
iemand wordt opgetild
en verderop neergezet
uit zijn hoofd steekt een voet

rol je verhaal op en leg het naast je neer
een toeschouwer zal het voor je weggooien

de huizen maken zich los van hun straat
een vogel verandert in een zwerm

the noise of just a body

you are at your best
when you see where you stand

your heart the drum of your philosopher
who knows better but cannot speak
stomping around like the fat neighbor upstairs
on his way to solutions in the fridge

wrap up your story
and put it down next to you

in the dance there's a moment
when the dancers don't move
but the dance continues in their eyes
someone is lifted up
and then lowered down a little further away
a foot sticking out of his head

wrap up your story and put it down next to you
a spectator will throw it away

the houses separate themselves from their street
a bird turns into a flock

schutting

ik ben een mens
ik mag vergeten
hoe de weg onder onze voeten zich vormde
lang voordat we konden lopen

ik was een voorouder
die niet zoals de rest
's nachts gerust ging slapen

mijn familie liet hier iets achter

ik ben een mens
ik zal getuige zijn
van onze terugkeer naar de grond

van onze handen die van de toetsen glijden
zich sluiten om de steel van een hamer

vanavond zit ik stevig in mijn tijd
die een stijve nek heeft van het omkijken

ik zie kinderen bouwen en breken
op witte stoeltjes wachten tot de vis komt
de eikels optellen tot een strenge winter

ik laat de weg achter
zoals mij verteld is

fence

I am a human
I am allowed to forget
how the road formed under our feet
long before we could walk

I was an ancestor
who unlike the rest
did not go to sleep peacefully at night

my family left something behind here

I am a human
I will be witness
to our return to the ground

to our hands gliding off the keys
closing around a hammer's handle

tonight I sit solidly in my time
that has a stiff neck from looking back

I see children building and breaking
waiting on white chairs till the fish come
adding up the acorns to a harsh winter

I leave the road behind
as I've been told

voor de boeg

de boten houden zich stil
tot het eiland hen gevonden heeft

in hun dromen ontwerpen de roeiers het land
voelen hoe hun tenen het zand raken
zien hoe de schildpad rechtsomkeert maakt

in hun hoofd ontwaakt het vermoeden van een stad

ze zien waar een groep vogels afbuigt
hoe de golven hun schuim verdelen
stapels wolken het eiland verraden

ze staan rechtop zodat de wind door kan waaien
omdat er niets meer is dat tegenhoudt

ahead of the prow

the boats stay still
until the island has found them

in their dreams the rowers design the land
feel how their toes touch the sand
see how the turtle turns itself around

in their head the view of a city awakens

they see where a group of birds branches off
how the waves separate their foam
heaps of clouds betray the island

they stand tall so the wind can blow through them
as there is nothing left that gets in the way

FIELD NOTES

Writing Bewilderment into Wonder

Poetry is a form of storytelling. As such, a poem can weave itself into the fabric of stories, ideas, and conceptions that shape our lives. Poetry can help to change the dominant stories of a time, and this time, many feel, is in dire need of a new set of stories to move towards a more sustainable future.

In my view, poetry is always connected to the world, the environment, in which it is written. Poets and writers can be the 'collective memory' of a place or of a group of people. Although some poets may be inclined toward an 'ivory tower' position, poetry is in most cases shaped by and in turn sometimes serves to shape the world. "Landscape is loud with dialogues, with storylines that connect a place and those who live there" (Whiston-Spirn 2008, p. 54). Poetry uses the stories from these landscapes about the land and the people and animals who live there, and in turn also creates landscapes—or places—of its own.

To me, being a poet means writing stories or creating 'storyscapes' (Viljoen and Van der Merwe 2004) that help people remember their connectedness to themselves, to each other, and to the earth. To remember: to realize anew that you are a member, an integral part of an interdependent web of life.

I like Thich Nhat Hanh's notion of 'interbeing' (2007). No living being is a self-contained entity; no one is separate. Yet people can feel deeply separate and alienated, a feeling that, in my view, is at the root of many of today's problems, notably the climate crisis. When people feel disconnected, the earth becomes a thing to them, a mere commodity exploited for economic, or at best, leisure reasons. Earth is there to serve our needs. This way of thinking can lead to a careless or even downright destructive attitude towards earth that by now we can see the consequences of. If on the other hand, people feel connected and experience all of life as one, then they will automatically treat others, themselves, and the earth with respect and reverence, and may realize that if you do damage to someone or something, you are in fact doing damage to yourself.

Stories, I believe, can help to heal the severed connection many of us are trapped in today. They can do this in a direct, engaged, activist kind of way, or take a more indirect approach. My poems are not there to give directions, nor do they present final answers, not only because I do not have those answers, but also because I don't believe in telling people what to do. I try to use my own bewilderment and my own questions, and share them with the reader in order to start up a kind of conversation. By means of writing I aim to bridge the gap between this confusion and the sense of unity and wonder that I know is also available to us. I try to build that bridge for myself and for others in each poem, whether it deals with nature, relationships, self-doubt, history, or anything else.

To me, this is at the heart of ecopoetry, an attempt to reinstill a sense of awe at the beauty and intelligence of nature, which is also our own. We are part of nature and nature is part of us. Poems about people, therefore, are poems about the web of life as much as poems about rocks and streams, or poems that deal directly with the climate crisis, for example.

My poems try to give people an inkling of how they can look in amazement at what might have seemed ordinary before; a glimpse into a more enchanted life. I choose my words and images in such a way that they might touch the reader in a place where a possibility lies dormant, an opportunity for a more connected, inspired life. And although I try to stay compassionate, I do judge and I do have ideas about what I think is right or wrong. The word 'eco' is not exactly a neutral label! However, I do not tell my readers how to feel or what to do, but rather trust them to form their own ideas and conclusions.

My book *Vrije uitloop* (Free range) is a journey from our most outrageous behaviors towards a more integrated way of being in which we are able to blend in, and become one with nature and other living beings, and be aware of the sacred within everything and everyone. Aware that we are already home.

— Saskia Stehouwer

Hanh, T.N., *The Art of Living. Peace and Freedom in the Here and Now*. Narrated by Edoardo Ballerini, Gabra Zackman. HarperAudio, 2007.

Viljoen, H., and Van der Merwe, C., editors, *Storyscapes. South African Perspectives on Literature, Space and Identity.* (New York etc.: Peter Lang, 2004).

Whiston-Spirn, A. "One with Nature" in Ziady, R. DeLue and Elkins, J., editors, *Landscape Theory*. University College Cork Art Seminar Series. (London/New York: Routledge, 2008), pp. 44-64.

For a new year

we needed a new kind of Bible not so much a testament as a ball of twine to be unraveled opened something linear yet undirected something beyond a ring-tone and finger-swipe to focus our attention something as vaporous as a cloud yet casting a shadow on the very ground we walk on while we consider how many haircuts it takes to feather a pillow or how the storm drain at the corner of Putz and Montana in Cincinnati is the final resting-place for misplaced car keys how it's a portal for errant raccoons how during autumn rains its grillwork resembles a coffee filter soggy & rank with leaves how at that corner with no school crossing-guard the storm drain is an arbiter of flow is this where the twine will lead us and will we find something to believe in

— Joel Thomas Katz

Parables of Consciousness: Guide to Vrije uitloop
by Saskia Stehouwer

In reading and understanding the poems of Saskia Stehouwer, it is helpful to approach each poem as a Parable of Consciousness, a lesson set in everyday experience. However, she has said it is not a lesson 'waving a finger' but rather an opportunity to consider and learn by seeing something in a new or different way. The poet prefers to 'show, not tell'.

The traditional notion of parable—a simple story with an important, even transformative lesson set in everyday experience, customarily found in the Christian Gospels— would direct you to something her poetry is not. And if her poems even have a story, it may not be all that simple. Nonetheless, there is a learning that is offered within the narrative framework of her poems. The parable in Saskia's hands takes the reader into the illuminating realm of consciousness. It is that territory of poetry where the reader is presented with an all-encompassing reality beyond ordinary understanding, with telling insights into the complexities of the human condition and the condition of the world that humans inhabit.

The subject of *Vrije uitloop* is the ecosystem of humans and their environment, or in Saskia's words, "the 'connection' of humans to their environment and each other; both relationships are equally important, I believe". This is why she states, "It is really poetry about connectedness".

Dutch Contribution

The Parable of Consciousness is an effective form of writing for examining and understanding the extraordinarily complex and difficult circumstances of our time and how we humans deal with them. As used in Saskia's poetry, this form is oriented toward providing context over content—the focus is understanding, not telling others what to do—which appears to be a realistic and pragmatic path toward helping humankind and the environment. This form benefits from the remarkable combination of the pragmatic and insightful found in Dutch culture with a particular expertise in the internal world and external world of human endeavor, present in the art, science, and philosophy of the Netherlands.

Saskia's poetry is but one example. Although not intentional on her part, Saskia transforms the traditional parable. She gives new life to it just as she has done in her re-invention of the traditional Dutch form of a proverb called the *spreekwoord*, which is found in visual and literary art from the seventeenth century. She creates her own aphorisms in the manner of the old ones. For example, the poem "Now" from her first book *Wachtkamers* (Waiting Rooms) concludes with "you need the autumn to get through the winter". (See page 95 in Field Notes for more examples.)

Saskia is very much the modern Netherlander who has transformed traditions of her culture's past into something new and significant—but without simply rejecting the old for the new. She appears to follow the model of the Dutch twentieth century artist Piet Mondrian, who grew up in a Calvinist home and began his career as a landscape painter, but whose work became transformed through his embrace of Theosophy and Eastern philosophy and the development of his personal style of pure abstract art. And as seen in the later work of Mondrian, he retained his propensity for singular devotion and the presence of the Dutch horizon in his canvases, however abstract—signature qualities from whence he came.

The same is true for Saskia. The lessons of the parable and *spreekwoord* are drawn from her traditional upbringing in the Netherlands. However, they are delivered and experienced in a highly personal form of poetry that belongs to the twenty-first century.

As such, it is important to point out that the 'lessons' from Saskia's poetry are offered on the premise that it is up to the individual reader to respond and decide what to do or not.

Consciousness

Consciousness in this sense serves as the context for the reality of these poems, both in what they convey to the reader and in what the reader discovers in them. In other words, consciousness provides an approach to the experience of the poems.

Consciousness encompasses the full range of human experience on levels of the physical, mental/emotional, and spiritual. The whole person is considered from direct perception of what is seen and felt (through the senses) as well as awareness of the world beyond the content of perception found in the psyche and the states of individual and collective consciousness as described by psychiatrist Carl Jung. That includes, for example, the ego at play, archetypes, and the goings on of the Shadow World.

Consciousness in this context may also be elucidated through other modes of understanding, such as the concept of Myth offered by Joseph Campbell from his work in comparative religion and literature. Another is the teachings of David R. Hawkins with his expertise in consciousness and mystical experience applicable to body, mind, and spirit in the fields of integrative medicine, psychiatry, and spirituality.

It can be valuable to consider these dimensions of consciousness in reading Saskia's poems (or in experiencing any work of art). For her work, in particular, which can appear puzzling or mysterious, thinking of her poems as Parables of Consciousness can help clarify and illuminate. For example, the reader will encounter in her poetry what seems like a dream, something quite surreal, a product of the imagination. Yet however strong that impression may be, the poet offers the reader a living dream-like scape of being awake in everyday experience.

By viewing her poetry as existing in the realm of consciousness, the reader is better able to negotiate the puzzling or mysterious nature of her imagery, phrasing, metaphor, etc.

The poet challenges the reader to go beyond ordinary ways of thinking, the usual and expected formulations.

Saskia shuns the templated phrasing of the sound-bite or tweet, or the simple symmetrical couplet. She has said: "I don't want to deliver bite-sized chunks" ("*Ik wil geen hapklare brokken afleveren*"). She sidesteps those tropes we consume and accept because they are familiar and tell us what we want to hear, the ones that confirm our perceptions and the positions we hold and rely on.

She transports us beyond that limited mindset, enabling us

to learn or imagine something more telling and insightful, something new that the reader may not have considered before.

— Robert Perry

++++

Het Spreekwoord & Saskia Stehouwer

je hebt de herfst nodig
om de winter door te komen

you need the autumn
to get through the winter

++++

[hij] kiest zelf de kleur van zijn boodschap
en weet dat brood bestaat
bij de gratie van boter

[he] chooses the color of his message
and knows that bread exists
by the grace of butter

++++

angst is rust die nog niet begrepen wordt

fear is peace not yet understood

[Sources listed in order of appearance—page 130]

About Ecopoetry

On hearing about our translation of Saskia's book of ecopoetry, *Vrije uitloop*, our poet friend Esther Kamkar asked, "Why ecopoetry?" Esther wondered why Saskia needed to apply that label when her poetry is about more than ecology or the environment. Her poetry resonates beyond that subject in many ways.

Saskia told us, "Ecopoetry is definitely not the perfect label. I would rather be known as a 'connected living'-poet but unfortunately that label has not caught on yet." She explains further,

> To me, 'eco' is not just related to the natural environment in the strict sense of the word. 'Eco' to me means being part of an ecosystem and relating to that ecosystem in a certain way. I believe that the way we treat our fellow human beings, ourselves and the earth are very closely related. To me it is all about feeling connected. When you feel connected, you see everyone and everything around you as worthy and sacred, meaning you will treat other people, yourself and the earth with equal care and respect.

With this question answered by the poet, I thought it would be instructive to see how Saskia fits into the broader world of ecopoetry. Conveniently, in an astute essay in *Poetry Magazine* (January 2016), UC Berkeley professor John Shoptaw asks the same question in the title of the article "Why Ecopoetry?" in which he examines the key features of this type of poetry.

According to Shoptaw, a poem rightfully earns the label 'ecopoetry' when it is both environmental and environmentalist. Looking at these criteria, let's see where Saskia's work stands.

Environmental?

By environmental, Shoptaw means first that "an ecopoem needs to be about the nonhuman natural world—wholly or partly, in some way or other, but really and not just figuratively".

Some but not all of Saskia's poems in *Vrije uitloop* are about "the nonhuman natural world". Among other things, in "A thousand ways to be human", we encounter sand that blows in the wrong direction and beetles that become lost; in "Cleft", the contaminated edges of pits where an animal has leaked out; and in "Hunt", human tools like hammers and air conditioners whose optimal physical design is based on woodpeckers and zebras, respectively. In "Bee", we see what it feels like to live in a hive-colony, and in "Becoming goose", we turn into one.

Shoptaw also states that ecopoetry is environmental when "it is ecocentric, not anthropocentric, though not without human interests or anthropocentric notions". Indeed, many of the poems in *Vrije uitloop* are 'ecocentric', yet deal with human behaviors and concerns.

The first poem of the book "A thousand ways to be human" is an excellent example. It refers to the slaughter of buffalo on the American plains very much tied to the human experience. And in the last poem of the book, "Ahead of the prow" (as well as other poems), the poet places the human in the landscape, the sea, and the land. And yet, a substantial number of poems focus on the human condition, and examine a variety of individuals with a compromised relationship with themselves, the world, and other humans.

In "Exit", a man with "a necktie for the evenings when he

almost goes out / only to crumble instead / a big hat for the tourist area / that he keeps angling through / as if wanting to apologize".

In "Fixed", a man with agoraphobia: "in your years of precision / when you rarely came outside / because you were held at gunpoint / few people got to see / how white your hair was".

From "In the clouds", people standing on windowsills and ledges who are contemplating suicide: "everyone down again in one piece / some hugged / others taken away".

While strictly speaking this latter category of Saskia's poems is not 'ecocentric', these are illustrations of Saskia's version of ecopoetry, 'connected-poetry' that takes a close look at the happenings in the ecosystem of our connectedness, the ways in which we are connected. For Saskia, it is all part of the same experience and concern—human activity and consciousness is an integral, if not inseparable part of the environment or an ecosystem.

Environmentalist?

In defining environmentalist, the second criteria for ecopoetry, Shoptaw states: "[The] environment of an eco-poem is, implicitly or explicitly, impacted by humans … not only thematically, in that it represents environmental damage or risk, but rhetorically: it is urgent, it aims to unsettle."

As stated in the last paragraph of the previous section, the poetry of *Vrije uitloop* is environmental with humans in a prominent role and in the way the poems challenge the reader to consider the human activity and consciousness that is transacted in them. Thematically, her focus is on the context of "environmental damage or risk" rather than the content. Again, her poetry is an attempt at understanding the human context, how individuals relate with each other and the environment, rather than examining the harm done.

In fact, Saskia has stated, "I prefer to show, not tell." Saskia will present the vicissitudes of the human condition, but it is up to the reader to respond as he or she will and decide what to do or not. She believes it is not up to the poet to tell or control what the public should do. Nonetheless, rhetorically, there is a clear sense of urgency with aspects that are unsettling.

Saskia would agree with Shoptaw who warns that a hazard for ecopoetry is didacticism. He elucidates:

> How can an ecopoem usher us into a new environmental imagination without teaching us a tiresome lesson? ... A familiar argument against didactic poetry is that it preaches to the choir. A poem should not preach, but it may teach the choir a new tune ... Of course, there will always be self-indulgent didactic poetry; a poem won't save the rhinos by telling us to. But I don't believe poetry that changes us, moves, unsettles, motivates us, or awakens us to the pleasures and wonders of the natural world is by definition bad.

As an antidote to didacticism, the rhetorical style of Saskia's poetry is often mysterious or puzzling, as she freely admits. She says she has faith her readers will make the extra effort or perhaps look at something in a way they hadn't before. She is a poet of the imagination with stream-of-consciousness imagery that is dream-like but usually exists in a living reality of everyday experience. The reader can have difficulty connecting the dots when they are sometimes set quite a distance apart, so to speak.

To help readers acclimate to her style and intentions, our fellow translator and project collaborator Robert Perry has contributed an essay here on page 91 in the Field Notes. Robert recommends approaching Saskia's poetry as "Parables of Consciousness" in which each poem comes with its own narrative within an illuminating, all-encompassing realm of consciousness, offering the reader telling insights beyond ordinary understanding.

— Joel Thomas Katz

++++

Indigo: Crisis of Good Intentions

Indigo is the color of aloneness, a state of separateness. The color of a material world in which we are imprisoned in our small selves, our own desires attached to matters ultimately of little importance or consequence. We are closed off from God, left to our own devices, in a state of fear and longing.

Indigo is the color of our time.

We are Lear on the heath, raging under a dark indigo sky, caught in a crisis of good intentions. Like Lear, we are trapped in a stormy dilemma—the waking nightmare of our own failings and those of others. We are flailing in the face of the dangerous results of the stubborn certainty of our good intentions.

The depths of smoky blue offer an opening, a way out to freedom and redemption, to a oneness. A way to embrace the whole to which all belong and discover our connection to the divine and our connection to everything and everyone.

In the smoky, swirling depths of indigo, there lives a hopeful something, call it light. The singular light that pushes through the indigo making its presence known. That light is choice. We have a choice. Even if we are enveloped in darkness, caught in this dilemma, we have the ability to choose, and despite all, to be positive and say yes to life.

The opening is always there for us to walk through and find our niche in that ecosystem, and with that understanding, help us to learn how to live and relate to that world and to those who live there with us.

— Robert Perry

The thoughts shared above are about the cover image of *Indigo*, a watercolor painting by Elsie Franken-Holt. The painting is an Anthroposophical art therapy training exercise to learn about the principles of the color indigo. Source: *Colour* by Liane Collot D'Herbois (Schneider Editionen, 2016).

++++

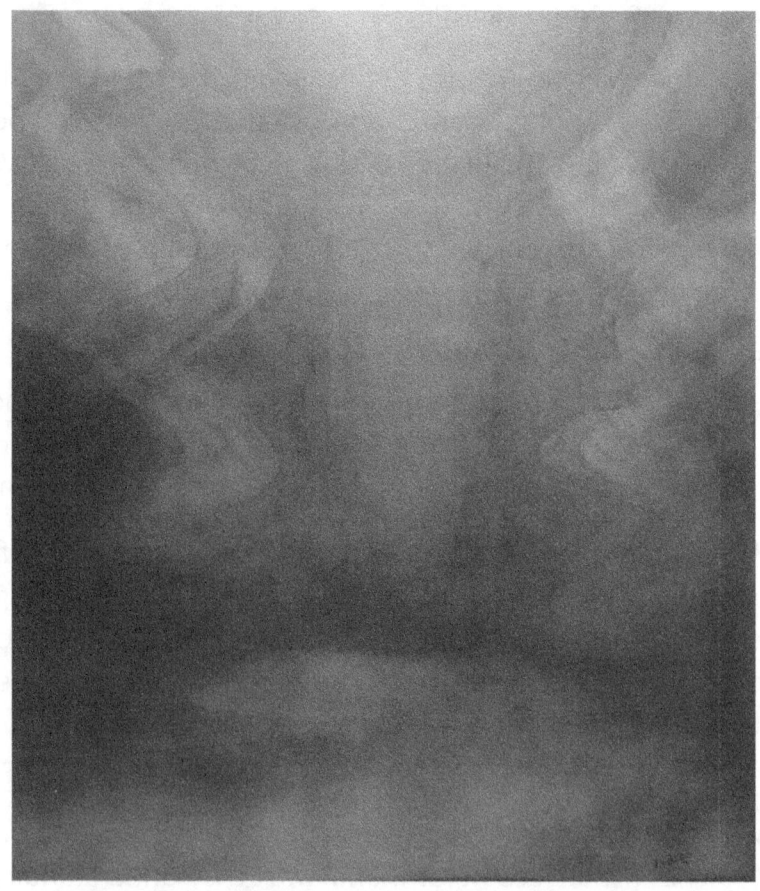

Indigo, a watercolor painting by Elsie Franken-Holt

A Conversation:
Poet-Translators of Vrije uitloop
Joel Thomas Katz, Robert Perry,
and Saskia Stehouwer

About Getting Started and the Dutch Language

Saskia:
Could you tell me the reasons why you decided to embark upon this project?

Robert:
Yes, absolutely. Well, it started with Joel.

Joel:
Yeah, it's my fault. I went to Perdu (a poetry bookshop in Amsterdam) where I found your book, Saskia, and Ingmar's [Heytze] to translate. That's how our first book *iets anders | something else* started. Then Saskia came along with a new book *Vrije uitloop* (Free range). You sent us copies and I immediately started translating it.

Through *iets anders | something else*, I learned how to read you, at least on the page. So for me, I wanted to build on that. With understanding the person behind the poems, I wanted to learn something more, a worldview, perhaps.

Saskia:
Why did you become so fascinated with the Dutch language?

Joel:
This gets back to my walking into Perdu and asking Peter Prins: Where's the poetry section? I was looking for a thin book,

first of all. And my other question: What is this poet saying?

I found I could pick out a few words. I thought: it's this intriguing cousin, a very close cousin of English that one could almost understand on its own, but not quite. It's like you're listening to somebody and they're just out of earshot. And you want to know: *What is the person saying? What are they trying to convey? Where are they coming from?*

And the sonics, the sound of the language itself, was very appealing to me. There's something I liked about it. All those interesting sounds like s-c-h, and the guttural g.

Robert:
For Joel and for me in my own way, our passion for the Dutch language is instinctual. For Joel, the minute he got *Vrije uitloop*, he started translating it without a thought about the implications of where this would lead us.

Joel:
It wound up being more than a weekend hobby. Right? (Laughter)

Robert:
I said to Joel: you know, this means there's going to be a book. And you do realize there are 34 poems to translate and that means we'll probably do essays to go with the translation as we had done with *iets anders | something else*. So now here we are months later with exactly that.

Process of Maturation

Saskia:
I think it's also been, apart from all the other things, a process of maturation. First you scraped the surface and then you

were really digging in. I can see you're getting better [at translating my poetry] and it's really exciting.

Robert:
We've become familiar with you and Joel's command of the Dutch language really improved incredibly, especially with the second book. About our email exchanges in Dutch, I ask Joel, do you understand everything we're saying?, and he says yes.

Joel:
Well, 90%.

Saskia:
That's very good. A real accomplishment.

Robert:
So as far as getting us into *iets anders | something else* and *Vrije uitloop* for that matter, I'm blaming it all on Joel. (Laughter) He started translating, so here we are. But of course I was happy to go along for the ride. I love Dutch and these are perfect titles to have for Dutch Poet Press. In fact, I've enjoyed the whole enterprise, where it's led us, like right this minute, conversing with a real live Dutch poet. And traveling to Holland and doing our reading together, meeting your friends and family. Wow!

For me, I've loved the sound of the Dutch language from the start when I first went to Holland during my college years—like when I heard it spoken at my cousin's house in Naarden (near Amsterdam). Also being very visual as an artist and designer, I enjoyed seeing the language everywhere I went—at the train station, on the trains, in the streets, on the money, books, postage stamps, you name it.

I just loved the look of it. That's why I decided the cover for *iets anders | something else* should have a typographic design. It made sense for a book of translation—it's about language.

It also helped to have taken Dutch classes at UC Berkeley and then go to Holland and use the language and see the art and design. It all flowed together—the art, language, and culture. Of course that included poetry. Remco Campert became my hero. That led to my choosing Dutch Poet Press for my press name.

Poets Who Translate

Saskia: I want to know, does it make it easier to translate poetry when you're a poet yourself?

Joel:
Yes, definitely, because if you're a fiction or nonfiction writer, you may not be quite as conversant with some of the tools and techniques that poetry uses. You're not necessarily going to pick up on the sound of it, or the metaphor. And you may not pick up how a poem can sound a little odd in the original.

Here's where you try to convey that sense in the English, because that's the experience the Dutch reader is going to have in the original, saying to him or herself: hey, wait a minute, this is a little odd … I don't know what's going on here. So instead of providing a sanitized or straightforward rendition in English, you try to give the reader of the English that same experience. As a poet, it makes it easier to negotiate all this. It improves our translation, too.

Saskia:
Yeah. That has been a pretty central thing, hasn't it?

Robert:

Yes, I think it's just part of you [as a poet]. You're apt to be more sensitive to all the dimensions of the poetry you're translating. You have the capacity to understand much better because you tune into all those other dimensions resonating there. As a poet, you feel you're getting closer to understanding the poem.

Translation as a Profession and Art Form

Joel:

Saskia, what do you mean when you asked us: does a professional poet-translator have the proper detachment or something like that? You also asked whether we see translation as an art or as a profession? A craft?

Saskia:

Yes, I wanted to ask about maintaining a professional detachment when you're translating.

Joel:

That is a very interesting question because Robert and I have been attending regular workshops with a group of literary translators who meet once a month here in the San Francisco area. They translate works of literature—poetry and fiction. That is their profession. It's what they do for a living. So, it's helpful for us because they really know how to translate. We learn a lot from them. In fact, they've told us that we're serious professionals, too, in our own way. Which was nice to hear.

Saskia:

Yes, I think so, when you see a good translation, it's a work of art in itself. At the same time, it's something that demands an incredible skill like a craft, something that an artisan would do.

Robert:
Yes, it is an art and I think the art makes it a profession so that translation is your *métier*. What is the Dutch word for that?

Saskia:
Vak. So we agree on translation being an art form, but one that also requires the skill of an artisan.

Translating with Two Things in Mind

Joel:
We often translate with two things in mind. The first is we make sure that we're looking at the text and translating what's there. The second actually comes from some advice we've been given from our workshop of professional translators, from a woman named Katie Silver. She suggests that it's really okay to diverge from the original in order to get the true feel and intent of the poem in our own language. This means we might have to use different words, structure, and patterning.

Saskia:
That's why it's an art form, and you have to do the original poem justice in the English, so it can be quite complicated.

Translation in Collaboration

Robert:
That's when it's helpful to translate with someone else. Joel and I are joined at the hip. Our mothers can hardly tell us apart. (Laughter)

Saskia:
I need to get one too.

Robert:
That's right. You have us but we are too far away.

Idiomatic Dutch

Joel:
Also, Dutch is so idiomatic. It's difficult because it looks so simple, and you think this is something right in between German and English, so I can figure this out. But since Dutch is so full of idioms, a lot of the time you can't rely on doing a direct or literal translation.

I mean, you really see this on Facebook when people post comments to each other in Dutch. It's extremely difficult for me, because the Dutch there is excruciatingly idiomatic. I read the words, translate each one, but I can hardly make out the meaning.

Something else that's challenging, and perhaps the most challenging, is that Dutch sentences and phrases are a lot more compact and terse. So most or all of what is intended to be understood is implied in just a little bit of text.

Saskia:
In English, it's the opposite. What I find difficult is that English is almost too overwhelming in that there is so much you are given and it's such a flexible language. You can go anywhere, you can make new words, you can change nouns into verbs, etc. And it's just, almost too much. English is just too easy in a way, too forgiving maybe.

Three Language Nerds Working Together

Robert:
Well, this is what's really nice in our working together with the poet. You get to know the artist's intention. I mean, it's wonderful that you're alive and we can talk to you and you're willing to listen and answer all our questions.

That's so, especially this time around, because you are a regular contributor, an integral part of the collaboration. When Joel and I have our weekly translation session (usually Friday mornings), we sit at a little cafe table and turn to an imaginary third chair. We say to each other … if Saskia were sitting there, I would tell her this and I would ask her that question. That is what we put into our email exchanges with you. You do a fantastic job of answering those questions and you seem to enjoy explaining and elucidating everything we ask.

Saskia:
I really like them because the questions, like the rest of the discussions, they're getting more and more fundamental and I have to think harder all the time in order to come up with an answer at all. And it's really nice for me too because it helps me reflect on what I'm doing. I think it makes us all into better readers, if not translators. Or even poets!

Robert:
It does seem like you love language just as much as we do. And that's very helpful. For us, it feels really quite miraculous you give us the time and you're willing to do this project. We ask ourselves: how did this happen at all in the first place, that Peter Prins at Perdu recommended your and Ingmar's

book to Joel, and then the two books and Joel found me. And we continue to get along swimmingly through the first and now the second book. You've been so cooperative and the enjoyment and learning keeps growing and growing. As Joel and I tell people, after more than two years, we are still talking to one another.

Saskia:
Yeah, it's quite amazing. I'm really honored by all the time and effort you guys are willing to spend on my poetry! We all three like language, right? We are language nerds and we can have discussions about one word. That's great. I really like that.

Distance between the Dots: Saskia's Approach to Writing Poetry

Joel:
You have mentioned and we have read that people find your work mysterious or puzzling. In a way, the reader has to connect the dots but the dots are quite a distance from each other. Therefore, the reader of your poems has to make huge leaps shifting from one image to another.

Saskia:
I think that was very witty of you, Joel, that the reader has trouble connecting the dots with notable distance between the dots.

Joel:
You have said you don't like to write in "little, nicely digestible chunks", right? Where do you think your style of writing comes from?

Saskia:

I don't know. That's a question that's really hard to answer. I would say that it's not intentional. The only intention behind it, I suppose, is that I try to express myself as honestly as I can. I've always written in a very intuitive way, not really thinking about the whole thing. Not foundering about on every word, not editing a lot.

I also have a lot of faith in the reader. I believe that the reader is quite able to figure things out and to arrive at their own interpretation, even if it's a different one from the one I intended. I don't really mind that. So I don't want the reader to be saved, or belittled, or feel that I have to be completely clear, or otherwise he or she won't understand me. I don't really mind if they won't completely understand me. I like it if people are somehow touched by the images and start thinking or doing something creative with them in their own right.

Having said that, this whole process [of writing and publishing my poetry], this has also made me realize that I sometimes make it a bit too hard, maybe. So I think I might try to become a little more coherent. I had already started to do that in this book (*Vrije uitloop*) to link the images a bit more than I did in the first book (*Wachtkamers*), I think.

So, more and more, I don't want to overwhelm the reader with images. I think I have to be vigilant about that. But also I don't want to write A-to-Z stories that people just read once and not really think about at all. I think for the most part people are able to handle things they don't understand at first reading.

Robert:
This is wonderful. Poetry is intuitive and things come up and you just write them down and you don't have control over them; that is, you get it out onto the paper and then you work with what you're given.

Ways of Understanding Saskia's Poetry

Saskia:
I also think there are more ways of understanding [poetry] than analytically, such as just understanding the words, because sometimes I don't understand the words myself, but I see the link between the images in a different way, in a more sensory, intuitive way, if that makes sense.

I think that the reader has more options than just the 'mental' understanding of the poem, and can come to some deeper impression or comprehension of it.

Robert:
Yes, your imagery resonates and has a lot more dimension to it, even dimensions. That's what I explore in my essay "Parables of Consciousness" I wrote for the Field Notes section of our book. I offer it as a guide to your poetry. I find there is a lesson embedded in your work, especially the ecopoetry. In being familiar with your biography, I thought of parables, even if your poems often don't have a regular narrative of beginning, middle, and end. However, I felt there is a lesson there within a narrative of some kind.

Saskia:
And I do [have a narrative], but I have a little trouble with the word lesson, I must admit, because it sounds too much like 'waving a finger'. I would say I provide some sort of inspiration that the reader can experience and react to.

Robert:

Yes, thank you. This will help me with the essay. I'll share it with you before we publish. However, I think there is a lesson in its purest form. I mean that you are offering some kind of learning. There's something there the reader can take with him or her that might prompt or guide change, or at least something for the reader to consider incorporating from your poems.

I say in the essay that you've transformed what you have learned growing up, like the parables of the Bible, into a different form of expression when you're telling a story that offers the reader or listener a lesson of some kind. The traditional approach get transformed. That's where the matter of consciousness comes in.

Stream-of-Consciousness

Joel:

Your poetry has a stream-of-consciousness quality. The poems seem to operate in the realm of consciousness with a loose narrative framework. For example, at times your imagery and such appears to come out of a Jungian Shadow World. This is how your poetry resonates in these other dimensions or states—and we can see why people say your poetry can seem puzzling and mysterious.

When one reads your poems, it can feel like one is in a dream-scape, but it's real. It's living in the present, not a dream. The reader can experience something like a fear, a deep fear, for example, and from that experience through the poem he or she can get a better understanding of how you as a human or someone else living in the everyday world deals with all those situations you enact in your poems.

Lessons in Saskia's Ecopoetry?

Saskia:
I think my poems convey how complicated it is to do the right thing. I cannot just say, okay, you human beings you do this and this and this and everything will be fine. Lessons like that are not there, because I don't have definite answers either. I do see a sort of connection between the images, but I'm not completely sure what the connection is so maybe you, the reader, can help me figure it out. That's why I sort of run from the word 'lesson', because that implies that I know how it should be.

Joel:
Right. So it's a process in which you are aspiring to learn something?

Saskia:
I'm learning and I hope the reader will come along and see what I find difficult and how I try to maneuver around and maybe they can follow me or take their own routes. That's more like it, I think.

Why Call It Ecopoetry?

Joel:
I believe you have heard of our poet friend Esther Kamkar. Esther wrote a blurb for the back cover of our book *iets anders | something else*. She asked us: why do you call your work in *Vrije uitloop* 'ecopoetry'? I think she asked this because ultimately it's all about the human experience of living in this world, not only about matters of environment or nature.

Saskia:

There are really two things I would like to say. And the first one is that 'eco' to me is not just related to the natural environment in the strict sense of the word. I think 'eco' means being part of an ecosystem and relating to it in a certain way. And I believe the way we treat ourselves, our fellow human beings, and the earth are really closely related. And it's all about whether you feel a connection or whether you don't. If you do, you will treat everyone, including yourself, people, and the earth with respect and care. And if you don't, you will just sort of trash around. So for me, there's no sharp difference between earth and people. I think while I don't deal directly with the natural environment in many poems, they do deal with the way we behave in relationship with nature and each other. And to me that's the same thing.

Connection Poet

So that's one thing. And second, why would I need the label at all? I thought about that. I think it's a good question. And I would really like another label, like 'connection poet'. That would be a great label, but it hasn't caught on yet.

For now I think this is the one that comes closest to what I do. It's important to let people know that this is what I'm about. It might limit their reading of the poetry, but I do want to stand for it. I want to make clear that this is my point of departure and that I write from there, although it's not supposed to limit the poetry. I don't want to do that in any way. The art aspect always comes first.

My main point is that I would like us to feel more connected to each other and the environment. And I think for now, this label is the best reminder of that.

Joel:
I wonder when people will see the notion of relationship that underlies all this stuff. And I think apprehending that notion is really central. Otherwise, people do the normal compartmentalizing, right? They could be very concerned about the environment, quote unquote. But they're very dogmatic and dismissive of people that don't share their view of how we're going to save the planet. And if you don't focus on this notion of relationship, then you're working at cross-purposes.

There's a lot of social shaming or value signaling that goes on quite a bit these days where it's said, if you aren't with me on this, not part of that program, then you're a part of the problem and you're not part of the solution. And I can go live this and feel very proud because I am part of the solution.

Saskia:
I think if people take the moral high ground, they are not connected because they have separated themselves from others. I feel that connection is really the basis of everything. If someone doesn't feel that connection, we will never solve what needs to be solved together.

Joel:
Actually, I've attempted to make this clear in my essay for Field Notes. I discuss an article on ecopoetry where you can see the various strands of this genre of poetry. I look at how they relate to your work. It seems to me you're operating on a higher level than other ecopoets with the goal of preserving the planet. I believe that is important to point out. Your approach is different than some other poets. As Robert writes in his essay, your poems are 'parables of

consciousness'. Not only are some others linear in their thinking day to day, but they think their opinions are worthwhile and everyone else's are just not worth bothering with. That is not very useful, productive, or very helpful. I like that you don't take that kind of approach.

Saskia:
It's not fruitful. Exactly.

No Manifesto or Polemic Here

Joel:
There are ecopoets who ... it's like they've written the poem before they start writing it. They put out a manifesto or a polemic where they want people to change. You may be interested in people changing, but *your* intention in what you write is to provide contexts or situations in which people can learn to figure out how to answer these questions or issues about the environment. That's what people can draw from your poetry, I think.

Saskia:
No, I don't think an ecopoet should do that. First of all, I don't think that anyone should tell people what to do. I just really think that's not okay. And the second point is, who am I to know? I mean that it would be really hard to write that poem and say, okay, this is how we're going to do it. It will solve everything. Just follow my lead. I don't understand that at all, actually. I think it's arrogant, and it also excludes people again, because then you're the one who knows it all and the others are the people who don't understand. So, no, I would never write a manifesto or something like that.

Robert:
Where does this come from? Is it just a matter of who you are as a human and a poet?

Saskia:
It's always a sort of combination of who you are at heart and what you've learned and what you've unlearned. I think I was raised never saying that I am the one who knows the answers and I write like that still, it makes much more sense to be among the others and question everything together. Like it's better to figure things out in your way and together, instead of telling people what to do.

But to answer where this comes from any more than that, it's almost impossible for me to say, oh, this is my culture, this is my education, this is me. That's really a question for you, because you're the experts on me now.

Joel:
You can't always know yourself or know what makes up what you are, what the influences are, because you're in the middle of it. You're busy being you.

Saskia:
When I studied Dutch literature, the first thing we had to learn was: whatever the author says about their work, don't listen to them. They have no say in this and we're the experts and we'll analyze it and we'll come up with our conclusions. And the author is of no importance. And I thought that slightly harsh, but I'll go with it.

Ecopoetry in Holland and the States

Robert:
Can we discuss differences between interests in ecopoetry

and the environment in Holland and Europe versus the States and specifically California?

Saskia:
I can be pretty brief on that. There is hardly any ecopoetry to speak of in Holland. I know two other people who engage with it and I know a few people for whom nature plays a prominent role, but they wouldn't call themselves ecopoets. And that's it. I've always been amazed by that. It's completely different than in the States where most people at least have some sort of rudimentary environmental awareness about them and they talk about it and write about it.

Robert:
Yes, there is lots going on here, especially in California and the West Coast. The traditions of Thoreau and Emerson in the East transferred to the West responding to the nature and ecologies of what's called 'California's Wild Edge' with Robinson Jeffers and Gary Snyder, among many others. I admire Gary Snyder very much because he took this tradition of writing and living further and deeper with his embracing the poetry and art and spirituality of China and Japan. This is what I grew up with—my heritage as a poet and a person who hiked and camped all over California since I was a child.

Joel:
Also the nature poetry of Mary Oliver from the East coast.

Saskia:
I think it's perhaps an Anglo-Saxon tradition because in England it exists as well. But we hardly have it, while the Germans have had a lot of nature writing. Interesting that we don't do this.

Robert:
I've heard Dutch people say in comparison to California—there is no nature in Holland. And you've heard the expression: God made the Earth, the Dutch made Holland.

Joel:
Yeah, but at the same time, when I flew out from Holland to come back to the States, from the plane I saw a whole bunch of wind farms off the coast. So there are people that are interested in the environment, water engineering and all that kind of thing.

Saskia:
There is certainly an environmental movement but there is hardly any environmental art at all as far as I know.

Robert:
Traditionally, you have landscape painting with an interest in the picturesque, but not the sublime, such as the Alps or the Sierras of California.

Saskia:
They (the Dutch) don't get swept away by our landscape. And they always talk about how other countries are prettier. It's a weird sort of identity thing here, to dismiss your own country.

Robert:
In modern Dutch art, Mondrian, for example, grew up with the landscape tradition but left to do Cubism in Paris. Then he got stuck in Holland during World War One when he really began to transform the Dutch landscape into his abstract style like those "Pier and Ocean" paintings with pluses and minuses. The landscape came from the outside and inside

and became this amazing art. In a way, Mondrian produced the equivalent of the sublime in this entirely new language of painting. He said the artist must paint what is inward, to create a purer vision of nature. I'm paraphrasing here but you get the idea.

Saskia:
Yeah, he made us see nature in a new way. That's where art becomes so interesting and important.

Bindweefsel | *Connective Tissue* Book Project

Joel:
Would you talk about your new compostable book project—*Bindweefsel … Connective Tissue*, speaking of connection? How did it come about and how does it connect to your poetry?

Saskia:
I think you already know the answer, but I'll try. I think it is by far my most direct engagement with, if you would want to call it that, ecopoetry or whatever it is. I've made all the paper from plants and written the poems by hand. What I want to do with this book, is what you said in the questions you've asked, making a really direct and intimate connection with nature in the form of poetry, in the broadest sense of the word.

Also you have asked me about whether this project has to do with my interest in permaculture, and it really does. I would say that permaculture is about creating something of a functioning ecosystem that is sustainable and can exist on its own. With this book, I've tried to create my own version of a book, becoming composed, becoming plant again. Having a whole process that is a cycle or cyclical.

The content of the poems is also related to permaculture in the sense of how we as humans can start to create an ecosystem on the planet and with each other. It also brings up the damaging things we've done so far and continue to do. So it's a bit big [in its vision and conception] and I don't want to sound pompous about it, but yes, I really liked the idea that I get it [all the materials for the paper] from the earth and I give it back to the earth without exploiting the earth in any way, without using stuff that would be detrimental to the earth or to anyone. And that's about it.

I also liked the idea that the poems will go away because the book will fall apart. People find it very hard to get this. That art can be temporary and transient and that we don't have to cling to trying to save it for eternity. And I think that's a bit weird. I actually like the idea that the poems will be in the world for a little while and then just disappear again. And they will be really vulnerable because they are subject to weather conditions and whatever happens to them. I like that. I like the fact that they are transient like we are anyway.

Robert:
Will you still record them and have them in another form?

Saskia:
No. In a sense they will just be gone. But they will still have been there.

Robert:
There's something very Buddhist about the idea of not being attached and letting them go. Nonetheless, I'm just thinking that it's still kind of a shame, but a lot of our life is that way.

Saskia:
Would it be a shame?

Joel:
There are those cultures who have people memorize their poetry, their literature.

Saskia:
Exactly. And I like that. Still I couldn't tell my friends to memorize the poems for me. I'm content with my writing all of them by hand, and by putting them each on paper thirty times, letting them decompose after that, it is a kind of meditation, a reverent act if you will.

Walking in Nature and the Writing Process

Joel:
Can you speak about your experience of nature in Holland?

Saskia:
You mean the Holland with no nature? I mean there is definitely nature, and I really like it, but people here say it is a boring place. (Laughter)

Joel:
You have talked about taking walks in nature.

Saksia:
I think it's mainly that when I'm in nature, I feel like a whole person. And when I feel like a whole person I can write. It brings you back to this sort of place of calm, no pretense … I think that's basically what it does. It's just there and it's not judging … It gives me a sort of connection. There we go again, connection with myself from where I can write.

Robert:
It's a good word. So what is the actual process of writing that you have?

Saskia:
I think the most important thing to me is to create a space in my head from which I can write. I mean, the writing itself will just come, but I have to make room. And that's the most mundane part of the whole thing, that I have to go from being a 'human doing'—which is not my term, but I like it—to a 'human being'. I have to start being.

I have to get the regular everyday chatter out of my head. And I usually do that by going for a walk. But if I manage to do that, then it will just come. And not that the poems all come out perfectly. Sometimes one does come out that way, and a lot of them just stream out and I don't have to do a lot with them. I'm acutally a pretty lazy poet. I don't edit my work very hard. I'm afraid the hard work is when I'm trying to clear my mind.

Robert:
Where do you write? At your place?

Saskia:
No, I never write at my place. I always write on the road, in a café or just on a bench, so I can sit outside. Just outside, but hardly ever at home. I edit at home. That's different.

Robert:
Do you write longhand?

Saskia:
Yes, always. I write everything longhand. Also I would write essays longhand versus typing.

Robert:
You use a pen and a notebook?

Saskia:
I always have that with me everywhere. I hear a lot, too. I'll hear people having an interesting conversation, then I'll just put that down as well. Like what people say on the bus. Or I see maybe some sort of weird sticker with some text on it. Everything can work, but I need to be open to it. At the risk of repeating myself, I need to be connected to everything to be able to process it into words somehow.

Robert:
Are you always writing then?

Saskia:
Oh no, it takes me weeks sometimes to get out of regular habits, and make the space I need to write.

Robert:
So you're generally very busy. You've had a lot going on in your life lately.

Saskia:
Yeah, exactly, I've been doing a lot. But I do write my, what I call, 'verbal diarrhea' almost every day. I have my big diaries where I put everything out on the page. I write my journals everywhere. I write them at home as well as outside. It doesn't really matter where I am, but I need to clear out the stupid things of today. And I make sure I throw them away regularly so no one will ever see them.

Show, Not Tell

Joel:
Let's go back one more time to this notion of how your poetry

of *Vrije uitloop* (Free range) is different than other ecopoetry. One of these strands is poetry that's didactic. For example, take your poem "Hunt". Another ecopoet may have the same mention of a slain rhino with the hunter putting his shoe on the animal's "lavish" neck, but the focus of the poem would be on telling us how to save the rhino or the like.

In *your* poem, you're not telling someone to do something. With you, it's just 'Here's the scene' as it is, just an example of something, an ingredient in the poem to make the reader think or consider the matter, perhaps gain a new sense of the situation or image presented.

Saskia:
Yes, exactly. It's a 'show don't tell' procedure really. Again, I much prefer showing something, not telling people what to do, because telling someone what to do creates distance and I don't want that.

++++

This exchange among the poet-translators Joel Katz, Robert Perry, and Saskia Stehouwer took place over Skype on January 11, 2019. The text provided here is an edited version of a transcription of the conversation with questions provided by the three participants in advance.

Alyssum

Alyssum sway in coastal wind
at peace in sunlight
fragrant on the Big Sur road
in a Carmel Valley garden

At my feet guiding me all the way
to the sea cliffs   the trail down
to the beach and blue horizon
before sky and ocean disappear
into mountains of mist

Ragged rock soften
cypress witness the weather
the history I carry home

Carry these rolling crashing waves
over the hills   across the San Joaquin
up the foothills to the sawtooth peaks
to Ebbets Pass   to glittering meadows
to the stark face stone jaw of the Sierras

Likely to come up in conversation
campfire   coffeeshop   cartrip
can't help myself   the sweet words
about the dark-eyed junco
before breakfast   flow like rivers

All that I wish to share about alyssum
in the late afternoon when I finish
reading Saskia's poems   grateful again
   for what Joel found at Perdu
and brought to my attention

Again for this book   and my partners
in translation and the rest

      — Robert Perry

TRANSLATION NOTES

grasmaaiers | lawnmowers

The Dutch have a tradition of keeping a neat, manicured lawn. An example of the popular word in the Netherlands: *netjes*.

jacht | hunt

The Dutch word *royaal* conveys a generous or lavish size such as vast, large, colossal, or stupendous. Its English cognate "royal" is used in expressions like "That guy is a royal pain."

laat me je tweede helft zien | let me see your second half

For the poet, *zingende muizen* (singing mice) refers to the sounds of the little animals who make their home in the walls of the poet's apartment in Amsterdam.

wachtzet | waiting move

A "waiting move" is a strategy in chess that attempts to prompt the opponent into making a disadvantagous move.

kabel | cable

Cable here means a long length of charged wire, a cord that connects things, or a cable railway.

document | document

Lowercase proper names are used in the English to be consistent with the Dutch.

medaille | medal

In the line "let's approach it from the other side for a minute", it was in keeping with the tone of the poem to present a declarative sentence in Dutch as a suggestion in English. Also, *even* is translated as "for a minute".

gans worden | becoming goose

The phrase *voortanden verzagen* was difficult to translate. The poet offered "saw up your front teeth" which sounded weird in English. In this case, we agreed to go with this version with the idea of keeping the weirdness from the Dutch in the English.

viool | violin

While it is common in Dutch to use the verb *zitten* (to sit) as it is in the poem, it doesn't necessarily mean "sit" literally; instead it can denote a state of being with "is", for example.

het rumoer van zomaar een lichaam |
    the noise of just a body

The typical choice of "talk" for *praten* and "speak" for *spreken* is challenged here. It's a matter of following the poet's preference.

schutting | fence

The phrase "of our hands gliding off the keys" refers to the keys on a typewriter or computer keyboard. "Adding up the acorns to a harsh winter" alludes to Brabant folklore about preparing for the season.

voor de boeg | ahead of the prow

The poet had in mind Polynesian seafarers who can sense faraway islands from the features of waves, currents, and cloud formations. Nonetheless, without that knowledge, one could easily imagine the scene set in the Netherlands.

++++

Sources for "Het Spreekwoord & Saskia Stehouwer" in order of appearance on page 95: "nu | now" and "stappen in de straat | footsteps in the street" (*Wachtkamers*, 2014), "jacht | hunt" (*Vrije uitloop*, 2016).

ACKNOWLEDGMENTS

The poems "vast", "kloof", "viool", "bij", and "jonge ogen" were originally published as "avond", "kloof", "instrument", "kast", and "jonge ogen" in *Revisor*, Number 8, January 2015.

"hoogtevrees" and "gang" appeared as "ketting" and "gang" in *Het Liegend Konijn*, Number 1, 2015.

"daadzaken" was written for an art project about the 18th-century whaler Hidde Dirks Kat, about whom a collection of poems has been compiled by Peter van Lier.

"wachtzet" was written on the occasion of the 2015 NK Chess Tournament, commissioned by the Foundation for Chess and Culture in the Netherlands.

"voor de boeg" appeared in *De Moanne Monthly*, Volume 15, Number 3, June 2016 and was written for the Marboei Poetic Anchorages Project of the Friesland water-recreation organization Marrekrite and the journal *De Moanne*.

"schutting" was written on commission from Antoine Achten, after a stay in his De Kemp Bed & Breakfast.

++++

Heartfelt appreciation for their contribution to this book is extended by the poet-translators Joel Thomas Katz, Robert Perry, and Saskia Stehouwer to Elsie Franken-Holt for her painting *Indigo*; herman de vries for his sculpture *Le témoin | De getuige | The witness*; the Kröller-Müller Museum for displaying the de Vries sculpture; Jessica Nielsen for her tireless proofreading of our book.

Thanks also goes to our friend Esther Kamkar for her interest in Saskia's poetry and our project; Uitgeverij Marmer for allowing us to republish Saskia's poems; the Dutch

Foundation for Literature for their generous financial support; John Shoptaw (Continuing Lecturer, Department of English, University of California at Berkeley) for his insightful article "Why Ecopoetry?" in *Poetry* (January 2016); and Harry and Marijke Aiking for a tour of the Cruquius Museum (*Haarlemmermeermuseum De Cruquius*) and a discussion of water management and the environment in general. Harry has been an environmental scientist affiliated with Vrije Universiteit in Amsterdam for almost 40 years. (The Cruquius Museum looks like a castle fortress and a church, but in fact houses the world's largest steam-powered water pump. Between 1849–1852, this pump and two others turned the *Haarlemmermeer*, an enormous lake, into a polder where Schiphol Airport now sits.)

Cover and Interior Design:
Robert Perry

Inspired by the design of *Vrije uitloop*
produced by the firm Riesenkind
of Den Bosch, The Netherlands, with
a sculpture by Clara Pouderoijen on the cover.

Printing and Binding:
IngramSpark

Display and Text Typeface:
Caecilia Sans

Designed by Dutch typographer
Peter Matthias Noordzij.

Nederlands letterenfonds
dutch foundation for literature

This publication has been made possible with financial support from the Dutch Foundation for Literature.

www.ingramcontent.com/pod-product-compliance
Lightning Source LLC
Chambersburg PA
CBHW070612010526
44118CB00012B/1489